Six-Word Lessons for

WRITING BUSINESS PLANS

100 Lessons to Woo Investors and Avoid Deal-Killing Blunders

Ray Waldmann

Published by Pacelli Publishing
Bellevue, Washington

SIX
~WORD
LESSONS

Six-Word Lessons for Writing Business Plans

Copyright © 2015, 2017 by Ray Waldmann

Published by Pacelli Publishing
9905 Lake Washington Blvd. NE, #D-103
Bellevue, Washington 98004
PacelliPublishing.com

Cover photo by 123rf.com/profile_stokkete
Cover and interior design by Pacelli Publishing

ISBN-10: 1-933750-47-2
ISBN-13: 978-1-933750-47-7

Introduction

This book will help you produce a good business plan. It can be used as a checklist of things to consider including in a plan, and things not to do. It is not intended to replace the many published and online guides that go into more detail and offer examples of text you could use. The book is 100 short lessons, with explanations, on how to make any business plan, and thus any business, better.

These lessons are about the "production" of a business plan, whether written, outlined in a deck of slides, conveyed by PowerPoint presentation, or scribbled on the back of a napkin. Whatever the format, a business plan's purpose is the same: to sell your ideas and your business to your audience.

In many places I use the term "product" to cover both products and services, not only to save space, but also to convey the notion that a "service" can be a business's product.

Producing a good business plan can benefit a wide range of businesses, from small coffee shops, restaurants and retailers, to Internet start-ups, to manufacturing or software ventures with national or even worldwide reach. It can even help nonprofits and charities focus their activities and gain support.

This book is distilled from my experiences as a management consultant, corporate lawyer, entrepreneur, business executive, university business teacher, and member of corporate and nonprofit boards. Along the way I started three companies, wrote six books on business topics, produced business plans for investors as an early-stage company's CFO, and invested in several start-ups. At the University of Washington I taught business subjects, mentored student entrepreneurs, judged business plan competitions, and advised student teams working on projects for local businesses.

Acknowledgements

I'd like to thank my wife Mary, author of two Six-Word Lesson books on Public Speaking and Media Relations, for her support, advice and editorial help. Special thanks for his many improvements to the text go to our son John Waldmann, a recent Stanford MBA running Homebase, his investor-funded company providing management tools for small businesses. Thanks also to Jackie Livingston, Chris Porter, Terry Greve, and Steve Handley for their valuable reviews and suggestions. Patty and Lonnie Pacelli, in addition to being the publishers and our good neighbors, contributed many ideas and moral support. Needless to say, none of them is responsible for any "blunders" in the final product—they're all mine.

"This book is very thorough, complete, and well written. I spent several years teaching business plan courses at University of Washington and Seattle University, and I made significant changes to the course over time trying to improve the way I articulated the purpose of the business plan. I wish this book had been around at the time."

-- **Steve Handley**, instructor of business plan courses at University of Washington and Seattle University, advisor to early stage technology companies

Table of Contents

Do You Need a Business Plan?

1

Why should you write a plan?

A business plan provides needed information to investors and lenders. It can also help organize a start-up company, attract and motivate staff, convince customers and suppliers that the company will prosper, and reassure you that your business concept is viable. The key thing to keep in mind is that a business plan is fundamentally a sales pitch.

2

A business plan improves your business.

Imagine building a house without a plan—chaos! Producing a plan will sharpen your concepts, reveal gaps in your plans, organize your data and information, point out areas needing attention, and provide structure for company operations. View it as a "sanity check." Producing a plan is a useful discipline and worth the effort.

3

"Plans are useless, ... planning is everything."

This insight was expressed by President Eisenhower in 1957 based on his military experience, but it is also true for business. Don't get attached to a rigid plan, following it blindly. Instead, assess your organization's strengths and weaknesses, understand your opportunities and external threats, organize into a plan of action, and adapt the plan to changing circumstances.

4

Plans can benefit almost any organization.

Business plans are useful for any organization, not just businesses. Any organization, whether profit or non-profit, should occasionally evaluate its goals and plans, strengths and weaknesses, and financial resources. Government agencies, universities and schools, hospitals, charities, arts groups, and many other organizations can all benefit from business planning.

5

Plans don't all look the same.

There is no one "right" way to develop a business plan. Published and online guides provide useful outlines, differing in content, emphasis and style. Many offer examples of successful plans. So don't worry too much about topics, format, length, and less important features such as type style. Concentrate on telling your story the best way you can.

6

A business plan builds your confidence.

Perhaps you still have some doubts about the soundness of your business concept or your ability to execute. The planning process helps you to evaluate your business. As you plan, your confidence should grow that the idea is sound, the company is viable, your action plans are complete, and you can execute them. If you are not convinced, how can you convince others?

7

What did you forget in planning?

This book provides a checklist of the important issues to cover in a business plan and can make any plan (and thus any business) better. Use these lessons to make sure you cover all of the topics your audience needs. This book will also point out what not to do, helping you avoid common mistakes that could kill the deal.

8

There are alternatives to written plans.

A business plan is a concept, not a format. Sometimes you will find that your audience needs a complete written plan with lots of supporting detail. Other times just a few PowerPoint slides will suffice. One way to proceed is to produce the written plan, and then summarize it on slides. Or you can use the PowerPoint version as an outline for the full written plan. Use the method that works for you.

9

Get help when you need it.

You might need additional research on markets, technology or competitors. You may want help putting together financial reports and projections. You might need legal advice on the best way to structure your business. The experts are there if you need them. You may also be able to get help at no cost from government agencies, industry associations, trade groups, or other sources.

10

What are the plan's key elements?

Business plan guides agree that successful plans include an Executive Summary, then sections, as appropriate, on the Company, Management Team, Products or Services, Market, Competition, Marketing and Sales, and finally Financial Statements and Projections. Other sections on Technology, Patents, or International Expansion, for example, might be useful to fully describe the business. Just make sure the plan tells your story!

Start Selling with the Executive Summary

11

Your business plan's salesmanship begins here.

An old adage on how to give a speech—first tell 'em what you're going to say, then say it, then tell 'em what you said. This applies to business plans as well. The Summary is the concise preview of the plan, and it must be persuasive. The Summary must reflect the whole plan, including important expectations on growth, profitability, and return. All this in just a page or two!

12

Is the business's foundation really solid?

Any reader needs to understand the basic business idea in the first few sentences: What does your product or service do? What problem does it solve? After that, provide the context: Why is it exciting, unique or meaningfully better than existing solutions? Why didn't it exist before? Will the business grow? When will it be profitable?

13

Is there sufficient market for viability?

A basic question facing any business is the nature of the market. The Summary must address this issue up front, or the reader will not accept what follows. Your plan must not only address market size, segmentation and competition, but also your plans for marketing, promotion and selling. Preview these plans in the Summary to remove doubts about your focus.

14

Stress your team's ability to execute.

Many investors say they invest in the team, not the company. Convince the reader that your team can credibly and successfully execute these plans. Summarize prior experience, business achievements, connections, education, or any other factors that will assure the reader that the company can succeed. In other words, brag about your team as much as possible!

15

Will investors or lenders make money?

Individual investors and lenders may have different strategies, but they all want to protect their investments and make money. Be sure to provide in the Summary concrete reasons to invest in you business. For indications of how and when your investors can achieve their goals, they will look to financial statements, collateral, growth plans, profitability projections, and exit strategies.

16

Good Summaries convince readers to continue.

The Summary should urge the reader to want to learn more by reading the rest of the plan and discussing the opportunity with you. If the business plan is just one of many a funder sees, it must stand out from the rest. It must convince the reader to invest time and resources in investigating your opportunity further. Take the time to polish it.

17

Avoid complexity, jargon, wordiness and mistakes.

Make sure the Summary is well written, complete and concise. You must use the Summary to state facts and plans as clearly and succinctly as possible. Your Summary will probably go through several iterations as you develop the rest of the plan. Remember that your statements and data can be checked, so if you want to remain credible, don't exaggerate, embellish or mislead.

18

Don't use shaky or exaggerated financials.

Any investor, lender or other knowledgeable reader will significantly discount overly optimistic projections and financials. Exaggeration is an easy way to damage your credibility. Obviously you want to be optimistic, but don't make wild assumptions or statements that can easily be disproved. Recognize significant risks and doubts, don't ignore them.

19

The Summary previews reasons to invest.

If you are looking for funding, start writing the Summary by listing the reasons to invest. A helpful process may be to quickly draft what you think the Summary should cover. Then write the full plan, with all of the details. Finally, come back and revisit the Summary. This way the Summary will be closely tied to the text, benefit from the plan's analysis, and preview the important plan conclusions.

20

Executive Summary— the most important section.

Let's face it—many readers will only read the Executive Summary! As the reader skims, he uses the Summary as a first screening hurdle. This is where you have to tell the whole story in just a few pages, aiming to arouse their interest to learn more by reading the rest of the plan. You must capture their interest and hold it!

Describe a Winning Team and Company

21

Have you fielded a winning team?

Most funders think the capabilities of the team are among the most important predictors of success, so it's critical that your plan describe their capabilities and experience in detail. Other company resources such as staff, facilities, or websites can always be added or changed as required, but success will depend on capable leaders.

22

What is management's relevant prior experience?

Demonstrate the team's capability through prior experience. Has the team been through similar management elsewhere? Are there important lessons from other industries that apply to your company? Do you have a team of advisors or board members to help? Don't ignore failures—learn from them.

23

What is the company's growth strategy?

Companies usually have growth strategies, even if they're stated simply: add new products or services; open up new locations or markets; grow the staff or resources; develop new technologies; acquire other companies. What's your strategy? Is the business scalable? What will it need to grow?

24

Can the team execute the plan?

This is a key question—is the team capable of executing the action plans, performing the key tasks, and hitting the plan's milestones? Your plan must demonstrate that the answer is yes! Otherwise, the reader will conclude that you're flying blind and trusting in luck, good fortune and miracles.

25

Why should the investor invest now?

A favorite question from investors is, "Why invest now?" What has changed in the world that creates your opportunity? Is your company taking advantage of industry change? If the industry is stagnant, has a gap emerged among competitors? What new developments and technologies in the industry will help your business grow?

26

Who are other investors and advisors?

If you are approaching funders or strategic partners, they will want to know with whom they are going into business. The management team is part of the picture, but so are other owners or investors. And don't forget to mention directors, bankers, legal advisors, accountants or others who are involved in the business—they can provide legitimacy.

27

Your story helps explain the business.

Get personal—tell them your story! How did you get started in the business? How did you come up with the business idea? What steps have you taken to get to where you are, and what were your accomplishments along the way? Your prior experience and successes build your credibility--don't miss this opportunity to highlight them.

28

Your strengths, weaknesses, opportunities and threats

Consider employing an analytical technique popular in business schools and guides called SWOT—the assessment of your Strengths, Weaknesses, Opportunities, and Threats. Although you'll address these areas in greater detail elsewhere in the plan, give the audience this information upfront.

29

What are your company's competitive advantages?

Sometimes having the better mousetrap is your major strength. Does the company have a superior product or service, a significant technology, some protected intellectual property, a head start in a new industry, a protected market, significant long-term contracts, or other advantages? Do you have research or expert opinions to back this up? And how long will these advantages last?

30

Can you become a "lean start-up"?

One way to prove the company's viability is through the "lean start-up" process. The company grows from concept to start-up with limited funding to prove its core hypothesis, seeking full funding later. You might test the market cheaply by selling an early version of your product, pre-selling it, or giving free samples. This evidence can eliminate some investment risk and make your business more compelling for investors.

Will the Market Sustain Your Business?

31

Who are the company's target customers?

The first rule of business is "know your customer." Who buys your products or services, and why? What is the "compelling unmet need?" Are you selling products directly to consumers, through wholesalers or major retailers, or to other businesses? Are you serving a local, regional, national or foreign market? What evidence do you have that they will continue to buy from you?

32

How big are your target markets?

How big is the total market and what are your current and projected market shares? Use whatever data or market studies you have. If you have to estimate, be sure to say so, but always base your estimates on reasonable assumptions or proxies. A knowledgeable reader will quickly spot wild guesses or unfounded projections.

33

What are the market's key segments?

Every market, no matter how small, has different segments that have different needs and respond to different approaches. Gender, age, education, income levels, and location are just some of the ways consumers can be segmented. If you're selling to businesses, differentiate them as well. Cite sources and studies where appropriate. Don't make the reader guess what segments you'll target.

34

What is your basic sales strategy?

No business plan would be complete without presenting the sales strategy of your business. You need specific and realistic sales goals. You also need ways to measure success. This strategy should discuss your methods of promoting the product, identifying customers, selling to them, and distributing and supporting your products.

35

How will you implement the strategy?

State plainly and clearly who in your company will do what and when. For example, what management, staff, outside help, or commercial partners will be involved? What materials, equipment, resources and funding will you need? Spell out your plans, responsibilities, timelines, and milestones. And don't forget ways to measure progress— you can't manage what you can't measure.

36

Who will manage the sales team?

This is a key position in any company. An experienced sales executive can add significant credibility to your team. The sales leader can hire salesmen, develop sales techniques, find representatives and partners, produce compensation plans, find contractors and call centers, and find staff product support teams. Avoid a "do-it-yourself" approach if this is not your expertise.

37

How "sticky" are your customers now?

One measure of success for a company is "stickiness"—how difficult is it for a customer to change from you to a competitor? Will your customers lose time, valuable data or relationships if they switch? Are you core to a workflow that is difficult to adjust? This concept has broad application to many businesses where familiarity with the product, the delivery systems, even the salesman, make it less likely customers will shift to other suppliers.

38

Does market research support your strategy?

Have you conducted or commissioned market research? If so, provide some data and conclusions (without disclosing information that you wouldn't want a competitor to know). If you haven't researched the market, your plan could mention what you'll do to fill the gaps. Recognizing gaps in the business plan is O.K. as long as you have a plan to fill them.

39

Do you have key ongoing customers?

Investors want confidence that you know the market's needs. Mention your relationships with existing customers, prospects in play, and major customers you've targeted. If you can't use names, at least use descriptions, such as "a major national provider of...." Talk to potential customers, and if appropriate, report what they've told you about their needs.

40

How you'll execute the sales strategy

Good ideas need good execution. Be crystal clear on who your customers are and how you will reach them. What staff will be required? What about other costs? How much money will you need to hit your growth targets? The capabilities of the team must reassure the reader your sales goals can be achieved.

What Are Your Products or Services?

41

What unmet needs will you fulfill?

Does your product or service respond to compelling unmet needs? This is a basic question to be answered in your description of what the business offers. Did you base your decision on what to create, design, build, or sell by responding to customer needs? If not, why do you think your business will succeed?

42

What are your business's current products?

Describe and document your current products or services. Include ads, product marketing materials or spec sheets, screenshots of the product, etc. Use these concrete examples of how you communicate to customers. Don't pad the plan with excessive examples or detail just to fill space; put examples in appendices or attachments to the business plan.

43

Can you successfully handle business growth?

Most attractive business plans show growth, and keeping up with growth can be hard. What is the company's operating plan? Can the team handle product line expansion and growth? There is no point in having a better mousetrap if, once the world starts beating the path to your door, you can't deliver it!

44

What are your prices and margins?

Product prices should cover your cost of goods sold (COGS) and provide sufficient margin for overhead costs and returns on investment. What is the market willing to pay, and how do you know? What do your customers pay for comparable products or substitutes to what you offer? How do these prices differ by market segment, and how has that affected your planning?

45

Do you have protected intellectual property?

Patents, copyrights, and trademarks underlie many successful companies. Intellectual property is an important asset when companies are being acquired. Even in an age of widespread imitation, hacking and copying, your company should protect its technology and ideas. Make sure to explain why someone can't copy what you're doing, or how you will respond if they do.

46

Are you planning product line extensions?

You have already described your current product line, but as part of your product strategy you should outline potential product additions, modifications, improvements or other significant changes to your product. You can't grow without change; make sure your plan reflects your current thinking about these opportunities so your reader knows how you plan to grow.

47

How will you handle operational disruptions?

Every day companies face disruptions beyond their control--weather, strikes, facility damage, supplier failures, computer or power outages, etc. But the reader must be made aware of any special factors such as changing government regulations, contracts, subsidies or approvals, evolving product standards, or new product testing procedures or requirements that could affect your success.

48

What product risks face your company?

Some risks are inherent in any business, but readers need to know what special product risks your company might face. Are your products vulnerable to technology break-throughs? Are there low barriers to others developing competing products? Are your products subject to obsolescence? What long-term trends do you see?

49

What product support can you provide?

Significant product liability is a fact of life. Some industries, such as food, cosmetics, pharmaceuticals, and medical equipment, face unique risks. In many industries, product support and warranties assure customers that the company stands behind its products. Are there any product support issues peculiar to your business? How do you propose to deal with them?

50

Do you propose building a brand?

Think of all the products and services known by a brand name. We wear Levi's, use Kleenex, and eat our Jell-O while Googling for our news. Some companies aggressively oppose their product names becoming generic category names. But this just proves the power of the right brand. Is building a brand part of your business plan?

Can You Meet Or Beat Competitors?

51

What major competitors do you face?

Some competitors are obvious—those who offer the same products in the same market segments. Other competitors may not be so obvious. What about products or services that substitute for yours, or eliminate the need for your products, or disrupt the market in other ways? Make sure you identify actual or potential competitors as specifically as you can.

52

Is your product's value proposition clear?

What is your value proposition? Why do your customers buy from you instead of from others? Don't get too "psychological" about the reasons, just stick to easy-to-understand factors. If you can't quickly summarize why a customer will choose your product, it's unlikely you've found a path to "product-market fit."

53

What are competitors' strengths and weaknesses?

Analyze your competitors' strengths. What evidence do you have of consumer preferences? Are competitors offering better products, more choices, better prices, and more convenience? How do they stack up against you? What are competitor weaknesses? How can you exploit them? Are your customers "sticky," and can you build on this strength?

54

How will you compete against them?

Some ways to compete are under your control, such as price, quality, convenience, customer support, etc. But your analysis could point out the need for more radical steps, such as investing in research and development, redesigning products, targeting other market segments, or expanding into new areas or territories. These steps may be expensive, which is a compelling reason for approaching investors.

55

How do your product prices compare?

All consumers seek bargains, but do you want to be the low cost supplier? Selling below cost to build market share could look desperate. You may not be able to sustain losses; your competitors may meet or beat your price; lower margins may not be acceptable to lenders or investors. Be honest with your readers about whatever pricing strategy you pursue, and be aware of its consequences.

56

Product quality, convenience, and reliability count.

Price is not the only way to compete. Look at product features, support systems, purchasing convenience, product reliability, and other ways you can differentiate your product or service from the competition. Your SWOT analysis (see Lesson 28) should point out ways you might successfully compete in these areas.

57

Does competing require additional outside funding?

If you are tackling new markets, expanding production, developing new technologies or products, you may need substantial resources. Is this why you're writing a business plan? If so, you must make the case in the plan, explaining what funding is needed, how it will be used, who will be in charge, and your timeline of development.

58

Are new competitors over the horizon?

Don't be blind-sided by market-disrupting technologies, products, or competitors. If you know your industry, you may be in a good position to recognize and describe these threats. Be sure to convey your knowledge to readers who may not be as familiar with your industry as you are. You gain credibility and convey confidence that you can meet these threats.

59

Be honest about any entry barriers.

Often companies rely on perceived or actual barriers to entry of new competitors. Do you understand these barriers? If there are low barriers to entry, how will you deal with new competitors? Do you have the first mover advantage, and if so, how long will it last?

60

Can you consolidate with your competitors?

Consider acquisition of other businesses to expand into new markets, acquire needed products or technology, augment your team, build on established brands, or otherwise improve your position in the industry. Funders may back this strategy if they are convinced you can make a reasonable deal, combine operations easily, and emerge in a better competitive position.

Operations: Developing, Producing and Delivering Product

61

What risks accompany your business strategy?

If you have completed a SWOT analysis, you have already identified some of the risks you face. Competitors may copy you, consumer tastes may change, government support may dry up, major customers may go out of business, etc. The risks are endless! But if you have thought about some of them in advance, you will have a better chance of dealing with them.

62

Don't make your sales targets unreasonable.

If your targets are unreachable, failure and discouragement are assured. Stretch goals are O.K. if they're within reach—they will push the organization. But have a reasonable basis for any sales targets so your team can work productively and be held accountable. Both your readers and your team can too easily dismiss unreasonable goals.

63

Will your product promotion campaigns succeed?

The sales process starts with product promotion. Having the better mousetrap is worthless unless the world knows about it. What features of your product will you highlight in ads, websites, on social media, in spec sheets, at trade shows, in handouts, or other ways? Who will manage the process? What events or activities are planned?

64

Have you budgeted for product promotion?

Promotion costs money, but it can't be avoided. What is your budget for promotion? Are there guidelines in your industry for the percentage of cost of goods sold to spend on promotion? How much is enough? Can you afford it? Can you afford not to do it?

65

What is the sales team's experience?

If the team has been in place at your company for some time, then highlight their successes. Provide background on the sales team's prior industry experience, sales performance, and achievements. If the team is new to the company or industry, prior sales experience can be compelling. This is one of the most important parts of the plan—don't short-change it.

66

Are you organized for business success?

Include organization charts or other information on the company's operating structure. If you're a new company, describe what structure you intend to build. Outline the company's legal structure and its board of directors, subsidiaries, and offices. But avoid overwhelming the reader with too much unimportant detail. Put yourself in the reader's shoes--what does he need to know?

67

Don't forget PR to assist sales.

Public relations efforts pay off. Good stories about you published online or in the right publications are free advertising. Some people have a knack for attracting attention to themselves and their businesses. If you're not one of those people, then consider hiring a PR consultant. Make sure your plan reflects this decision and budget accordingly.

68

Product delivery is an essential function.

Product delivery and distribution--through retailers, online, or other means--directly touches the customer. You want this experience to be as trouble-free and pleasant as possible. How does your customer actually get your product? Customers' future purchasing decisions will be based on the impressions they form about you from their purchasing experience. Make sure it's positive.

69

Do you have any sales partners?

Teaming up with other, perhaps better-established partners for sales and delivery may enhance the customer experience. You can expand your reach into additional markets, take advantage of an experienced sales force, add more credibility to your company in its early stages, and perhaps even secure financing or support. Such partnerships could be significant company assets.

70

Operational details must not be overstressed.

Business plan guides often suggest adding sections about other operations topics, such as facilities, supply chains, production processes, inventory controls, distribution methods, customer service, call centers, financial controls, R&D activities, office technology, etc. Be judicious about what you cover—don't give too much detail that is not important to outsiders.

Putting it all Together: Compelling Financials

71

Stick to conventional financial statement formats.

Financial statements are where all of the previous information in the plan comes together. Your readers will expect to understand the statements without much explanation, so use "Generally Accepted Accounting Principles" when presenting the information. Save your creativity for other areas—financial statements need to be conservative and conventional.

72

Basics: cash flow, earnings, balance sheet.

Cash flow tracks the day-to-day life of the business, i.e., keeping the doors open. The earnings statement records and forecasts profits and losses. The balance sheet gives the past and future financial status of the company as of particular dates. Avoid unrealistic sales, earnings and asset projections (so-called "hockey sticks"). Most readers know over-optimism when they see it.

73

Other statements to increase your attractiveness

Two more useful statements for investors are: "sources and uses of funds" and breakeven analysis. The first supplements the cash flow statement with more detailed projections on where funds will come from and where they will be used. The second tells when the business will generate excess cash for dividends, debt payments, stock buy-backs, or other returns on investments.

74

Are your relevant material assumptions footnoted?

Your financial statement may have assumptions that need to be spelled out in the text or in footnotes. Let the reader know where information is available elsewhere in the plan, or where assumptions underlie your projections, let the reader know. If you don't, you could have problems if readers can later claim your plan and financials were misleading.

75

What risks are inherent in projections?

You can't predict the future, but you might have some ideas about the range of possible future outcomes. Business risks translate into variability in projections. If appropriate, you can present alternative forecasts based on optimistic, expected and pessimistic outcomes. You will help the reader understand the best and worst case scenarios.

76

Don't overwhelm readers with financial minutia.

One mistake frequently made in financial reports is excessive detail. Top-level entries should be consolidated from many subsidiary entries that don't need to be presented. For example, don't list sales to every one of your customers—just report sales in key or important segments. If more detail is useful, put it in an appendix or supply it separately.

77

Be accurate in your financial statements.

One of the worst mistakes you can make is to lie or make mistakes in your financials. If lies or mistakes are discovered (and most likely they will be), your credibility will be lost. Avoid even innocent mistakes or exaggerations. Forecasts must be realistic, believable, and accurate if you are to convince the reader. Otherwise you risk a major deal-breaking blunder!

78

Don't be surprised by skeptical questions.

Be prepared for detailed discussion of your financial reports and forecasts. This is normal back-and-forth procedure between those seeking funds and those with them. In your answers to questions, use facts and data, be respectful, and remain calm. Don't be defensive. Your ability to handle normal skepticism with skill will build the funder's confidence in you and will help close the deal.

79

Use professional financial advisors for credibility.

Early-stage companies can benefit from financial statements prepared by professionals. Later-stage companies with outside investors or lenders will likely be required to use outside accountants. Help your accounting advisors to understand your business and any unique financial aspects that should be reflected in your accounts. Make sure they're on your side.

80

Can you benchmark against other companies?

While benchmarking is not formally part of the standard financial reports, you can include data that compares your expected results with those of competitors, similar start-ups, acquisition targets, or other investments made by your target investor. Benchmarking can convince readers that your assumptions are reasonable and may help sell yourself and your company.

"The Ask" -- Goal of Your Plan

81

Use cover letter for "the ask."

Let's assume the purpose of your business plan is to raise money for your venture. The normal way to make "the ask" is through a short cover letter enclosing your plan. You don't want to include "the ask" in the plan, since you may want to use the plan with other readers. The cover letter allows you to tailor your pitch to readers and it absolutely must grab their attention!

82

Mention any connections with the recipient.

Most guides advise beginning the letter with any connection you have to the recipient—for example, "Your lawyer Harry Smith suggested that I send you this plan...." It is worth following this advice if you can. Otherwise you might begin the letter with a more general statement, such as "I believe our business opportunity may be of interest to you given your past investments in similar ventures."

83

What amount is sought and why?

The heart of "the ask" is: How much funding are you seeking and for what purpose? How will you use the funds? You must have simple, direct and unambiguous answers to these questions. It is not enough to respond with generalities like, "We intend to grow the business." What do you need and why? The answer must be crystal clear.

84

What company activities will be financed?

Spell out specific plans, with the costs and expected results. Are you going to hire more staff, expand into new territories, acquire or develop new technologies, expand product lines, or acquire other businesses? What results are expected? When will results be seen and realized? What financial risks are foreseen?

85

What is the company's pre-money valuation?

How much of the company will investors receive for their investment? They will want to know, discuss, and negotiate the "pre-money" (before funding) value of the company. Market values of your shares, conventional financial analysis, or benchmarking against similar companies will start the valuation discussion. You can get help from lawyers, accountants or others; even press reports may help.

86

Can you provide collateral or guarantees?

Banks will require notes, bonds or loan documents as evidence of the debt, and they will want collateral or guarantees from individuals to back the loan. This could come from you or your partners, if you have enough net worth. Don't give detail about collateral or guarantees in the "ask" letter, just be aware that in the negotiation of the loan these issues might arise and you will need answers.

87

What are your proposed exit strategies?

Private angel investors, venture capitalists and similar investors primarily want equity (through stock, options or convertible notes) that grows with company success. You should not only be aware of what your potential investor needs, but also how any possible exit strategies would play out. Will you be acquired, go public, sell out to a competitor, or some other exit?

88

Can you sweeten the funder's deal?

As you negotiate a deal, your funder may seek involvement in your company through a seat on your board, stock options or warrants, preferred shares, or other ways to sweeten the deal. New businesses with uncomplicated structures may not be able or want to respond to such requests, but later-stage companies with more complex structures can often structure a deal satisfactory to both sides.

89

Look for lead investors—"bell cows."

Investors like to be part of a group following the lead of a respected or successful investor. If you can find and convince such a leader, others may follow. Often the result is a group of investors, each taking a piece of the deal. This can make your financing round much more successful than holding out for one investor to provide all the funding needed.

90

The "ask" letter must be tailored.

Generic letters, especially those with inappropriate carry-overs from previous letters, are deal-breakers. Take the time to consider how to approach each recipient, and draft accordingly. Don't make the mistake of just changing addressees in a mass mailing list! And make sure names are correctly spelled and there are no typos.

The Right Presentation for the Audience

91

Goal: the audience considers your plan.

At some point you may have the opportunity to present your plan to an audience, whether it is a funder, a potential partner, a candidate for a senior position in your firm, or some other group important to your company. Depending on your audience's process, your presentation may be either before or after your full plan is reviewed. Don't insist on doing it "your way"--go with the flow.

92

Who's the audience for your plan?

A good business plan can be used in many different situations with different audiences. Some guides suggest using plan modules in different combinations for different audiences, as appropriate. But for most audiences, few if any changes to a well-written plan may be required. Just be clear in your mind that your audience is, and if you think changes to the plan are needed, make them.

93

What level of detail is appropriate?

You can look at a complete business plan as having three layers—a brief "elevator speech," a longer PowerPoint summary, and the full written plan. Each layer contains more detail and analysis. Increasingly, audiences are initially satisfied with shorter PowerPoint or other brief presentations to screen opportunities, but before making a decision they might expect a complete written plan with financial projections.

94

Have your business's "elevator speech" ready.

Develop a two or three-minute speech summarizing your business and the opportunity. You never know when you might have an occasion to speak briefly to a potential investor or an important audience. Some angel investor groups, for example, allow only a few minutes for each presenter to outline his company's plan. Your goal must be to pique their interest so they want to hear more.

95

Grab the audience's attention with PowerPoint.

Abstracting key elements from your plan for a PowerPoint or other presentation should be relatively easy. Keep the slides simple and easy to read—they must convince the audience to consider your complete plan and "the ask." Or you can reverse the process— use the PowerPoint presentation as your outline for writing the full plan. Either way will work and be successful.

96

Consider each presentation audience's particular requirements.

Tailor your presentation to meet the audience requirements. If you are presenting to angel investors, for example, stress growth potential, financial projections, and exit strategies. Be prepared to touch on these in the presentation, and make sure your written business plan backs it up with credible data.

97

Do you need personal financial statements?

Different funders have different requirements to ensure the safety of their investments. Banks in particular are interested in the assets of owners or partners, especially when they back the loan by personal guarantees. Venture capitalists and angel investors are less interested in guarantees, but they are impressed by the results of previous business ventures.

98

Protect all of your sensitive information.

Include statements on your plan that it is confidential and cannot be copied, but recognize that such restrictions are hard to enforce. Most investors and venture capitalists will not sign a nondisclosure agreement just to review a business plan, so don't expect it. Don't put competitively sensitive information in the business plan—just discuss it verbally or put it in a separate controlled document.

99

Keep records and notes of contacts.

If you are approaching more than one funder, be sure to keep good records of all contacts, conversations and status. You don't want to approach a prospective funder twice, or make a mistake about names, interests or other details. You might also ask your contacts for referrals--do they know of anyone else who might be interested in funding your business opportunity?

100

One final thought— enjoy the process!

If you are knowledgeable about your business, then describing it and discussing it should be easy for you. Be enthusiastic and confident! Don't be afraid to write or speak about your opportunity—after all, you know more about it than anyone else. There may be dry holes, but there can also be gushers—just keep drilling!

Contact Ray

I hope you have gained some tips on business plans, and I would welcome your comments. Please let me know your thoughts at
Waldmann@6WordLessons.com

Thank you and best of luck with your business plan and new venture!

About the *Six-Word Lessons Series*

Legend has it that Ernest Hemingway was challenged to write a story using only six words. He responded with the story, "For sale: baby shoes, never worn." The story tickles the imagination. Why were the shoes never worn? The answers are left up to the reader's imagination.

This style of writing has a number of aliases: postcard fiction, flash fiction, and micro fiction. Lonnie Pacelli was introduced to this concept in 2009 by a friend, and started thinking about how this extreme brevity could apply to today's communication culture of text messages, tweets and Facebook posts. He wrote the first book, *Six-Word Lessons for Project Managers*, then started helping other authors write and publish their own books in the series.

The books all have six-word chapters with six-word lesson titles, each followed by a one-page description. They can be written by entrepreneurs who want to promote their businesses, or anyone with a message to share.

See the entire *Six-Word Lessons Series* at 6wordlessons.com

www.ingramcontent.com/pod-product-compliance
Lightning Source LLC
Chambersburg PA
CBHW060612210326
41520CB00010B/1316